Why Would A Lovi

To Make an End of Sin.

By

Tony Baldwin

First Printing 2014

Publishers

Foggy Mountain, The Woodlands, TX.

and

Triune Group, Inc. Publishers, Marietta, GA.

ISBN - 13: 978-1514121580

ISBN – 10: 1514121581

FOREWORD

My friend Tony Baldwin has written a wonderful and insightful book on our Loving God. No matter if you are just getting to know the Lord or need helpful reminders of who He is and why we are here (like my- self) you will find this a good read. I have already started to share some of this wisdom and facts with family, friends and staff. Thank you Tony for being faithful.

David Wood, Executive Producer

The Resurrection of Jesus Christ (the film)

Table of Contents

Prologue

This book has morphed since I began writing it. Originally, it was supposed to be a conversational book that looked at difficult biblical passages and difficult passages in life-ultimately explaining them and encouraging the reader to begin studying the Bible for themselves. Since it was meant to be conversational, I omitted specific scripture references.

One thing I love about the Bible and is also a proof that it is indeed God's word, is how you can read the same passage at different times and God allows you to see different nuances that seem to be specific to your needs of the moment.

In writing this book, one passage; Daniel 9:24, came to mind but in a different way. "Seventy weeks are determined upon thy people and upon thy holy city, to finish the transgression and to make an end of sins, and to make reconciliation for iniquity, and to bring in everlasting righteousness, and to seal up the vision and prophecy, and to anoint the most holy."

This passage is usually looked at in terms of prophecy showing the total time allotted to Israel in God's time line. 70 weeks-or-490 years. 483 years through the crucifixion with 7 years remaining. Those seven years are the coming tribulation. This prophecy specifically deals with Israel and proves God is not yet finished with the Nation of Israel. In this light, there can be no substitution of the Church for Israel as some folks do.

This substitution has caused or helped to cause many errors in interpretation and also has al- lowed evil such as the holocaust. If God is finished with the Jewish Nation and they have no prophetic future, then some have reasoned they have no purpose or place in this life now. This allowed the church to not object in Germany as Hitler looked at and began his 'final solution'. It allows anti-Semitism to grow unchecked. I think it is allowing that viewpoint to begin growing again only this time from an Arab perspective. This will lead to another Jewish holocaust in the future.

All of that is extremely important. But it is not what caught my eye this time. The specific phrase I want to focus on is; 'to make an end of sins'.

When Jesus came to sacrifice himself for us and to be our Savior, he made an end to the *penalty* of sin. All who accept that Jesus made his sacrifice for them will be saved from their sins. But, there has not yet been an *end* to sin. Sin is still with us. We still sin, we still need to ask for God's forgiveness. He will forgive us based on the work of Jesus on the cross, not on anything we have done or could do on our own.

To make an *end* of sin. At some point in the future, there will be no more sin. It will be over. That has to be one of God's main goals in reconciling creation to himself. Having a creation that is without sin - for eve1more. Of course the pinnacle of the process is the Cross of Christ. The ultimate victory of the cross is an 'end of sins'. This is the Big Picture. It answers the big question that academics have pondered about for ages: 'why are we here?'

We're here to help God make an 'end of sin'. When you look at puzzling scripture, look at it in this light. How does this story or situation fit into the ultimate goal of the Lord? How does it help make 'an end of sin?' When you frame a Bible story or Bible situation like that you will find that suddenly it seems to make sense. You can see why God did or allowed certain things to happen. You can imagine how hard it was for God to allow certain things that the Bible dis- cusses, just as it is hard for God to allow certain things to happen in this world today.

God made salvation for us easy. He made it hard for himself. He did all the heavy lifting and all the dirty work. All we have to do is to accept the sacrifice of Jesus and we can be saved. The hard part is allowing Jesus to be Lord of our life. Yielding our desires, impulses, pride, etc. is not something most folks find easy to do.

I thought about using this information as the last chapter in the book and allowing the readers to have an 'ah-ha' moment. But I feel that the examples in the book will make more sense to every reader when it is framed in the light of the Big Picture of the Lord. If the book makes more sense to the reader then they will more likely follow my suggestion to begin studying the word of God for themselves. Why? To become secure and confident in our own salvation. The Bible tells us to be ready 'in season and out to give account of our own salvation-our own blessed hope-to others. In fact, that is the part we play in God's grand plan. He is allowing us to be the mouthpiece of salvation (alongside his scripture and fact based preachers).

Wait a minute. Sin came into the world through man didn't it? Yes, and there is a certain poetic justice in God using man as a partner in sharing his plan of salvation.

Heaven the eternal home of the Lord	It is assumed heaven has always been with the Lord

Angels	Were created at some point in the distant past. They were created to worship and serve the Lord in heaven. They were given free will which God knew they would abuse. God chose to create them anyway knowing the process of their sin and their temptation of man which would also come, had to be a part of the process in order to
The Universe as We know it	Was created to please God and to give mankind a central place of abode, the earth. It was also created to give the fallen Angels a place to go after they were expelled from Heaven
Hell	Created as an eternal place of punishment for the devil and the fallen angels that chose to follow Satan. Hell is at some place in the bowels of the earth.
Mankind	Created in the 'image of God'. While we don't know specifically what that means, scholars have speculated that God as a triune being, created a triune man with 'body, soul and spirit'. Man in his earthly body is created a 'little lower than the angels'. In our heavenly bodies in glorified form we will be 'above the angels'.
A universe where there Is an end of sin	A Universe as God designed it to be in his mind. A sinless universe where we and all the angels worship God willingly without sin and without the threat of sin ever entering into the universe again. A creation where we dwell with the Lord forever. A creation that pleases the Lord.

God's timeline to the place where there is an 'end of sin'. The red box shows

You can see from the timeline that we are a lot closer to the end than the beginning. We don't know exactly how much time is left before the rapture and the beginning of the seven year tribulation period. It may be twenty years or two hundred years. I lean towards a twenty to thirty year period based on a generational

view from the Israeli recapture of Old Jerusalem in the 1967 War with the Arabs.

After the seven year tribulation which culminates in Armageddon with the return of Jesus, there will be a 1,000 year period of peace with Christ on the throne and ruling the world from the temple in Jerusalem.

After that, Satan (who has been cast in hell during this time) will be loosed for a little while to tempt men again and unbelievably there will be some who choose to

follow him. This will separate the sheep from the goats for the last time.

Satan will be chained and taken to hell where he will spend eternity. His latest followers will go with him.

The remaining people will all be believers in Jesus and will spend eternity with him. The world will not 'end' but it will be changed, recreated in ways we do not fully understand. One change the Bible mentions is that there will be no more seas.

The heavenly city which has hovered over the earth during the thousand year period will fully descend to the earth and be a part of the earth forever. Men and angels will live with God for- ever. Sounds like science fiction doesn't it? It's not. This is a real part of our future. It will take all of this to get to the point where there will be an 'end of sin'. God didn't create the universe, the angels and man and cross his fingers hoping this all works out the way he wishes it. He knew in advance what free will would mean to the angels and to mankind. He knew neither could handle it and he created a path to cleanse creation that has fallen from his grace. It is through his grace that redemption became available.

To us, thousands of years are such long periods that we have trouble even grasping the concept of a time span that long. To God though, the Bible tells us that a thousand years is like a day. The redemption plan to get to a point where there is an 'end of sin' that takes thousands of years seems a near eternity. To the Lord, it is just a few days.

In the Garden of Eden Adam walked with the Lord in the cool of the evening. Can you imagine that? At that time of course, Adam was the only man. In eternity future we will be able to walk with the Lord again. There will be billions of us at that time and I am sure that God will some-how make each of us feel as special as Adam must have felt. No more sin, no more sin nature, nothing to embarrass us before the Lord. Just a blissful peace being in his presence. An awe- some reverence that pours out of us in word, thought and deed.

Heaven

As we transition from the prologue into the book I thought it would be a good idea to talk about heaven. There have been many complete books about heaven that are quite detailed. One I would like to recommend is by Jesse De Plantis; 'Heaven, Close Encounters of the God Kind'. While his title is an obvious play on the movie E.T., this is real and details the encounter he had when God took him to heaven. When he met Jesus, he was told to go back and tell everyone 'I am coming soon'.

I did my due diligence and checked out his facts against the Bible and I am convinced his book describes an event that really happened. It is not sensationalized and it was many years after the event that he finally wrote it down. It is a good read with lots of information.

The Bible tells us that heaven is 1500 miles long, 1500 miles wide and 1500 miles high. It is easy to assume with that description that heaven is a cube. I prefer to think of it as a pyramid with the throne of God at the peak of the pyramid where he is always in view and provides light to the whole city. This is in actuality the heavenly city that will one day descend and hover over the earth during the thousand year reign of Christ on earth. After the thousand year reign of Christ the heavenly city will fully descend to the earth and be there forever in eternity future. There is a wall surrounding the city that is 200 feet tall and has twelve large gates made of pearl; three gates on each side. Each gate had the name of one of the twelve tribes of Israel so they could be honored and remembered forever. There are twelve foundations of the city each of the foundations is a precious gemstone; jasper, sapphire, chalcedony, emerald, sardonyx, sardius, chrysolite, beryl, topaz, clnysoprasus, ja cinth, and amethyst.

The city itself was like pure gold, transparent like clear glass. There is no temple in heaven for the Lord and Jesus are the temple. The Lord and Jesus are the light of the city and there will be no darkness or night there.

There is a river of life that precedes from the throne of God throughout the city. On each side of the river in the middle of the streets on each side there are the trees of life which bare a different fruit each month (time still has some purpose. This is probably for use during the thousand year reign of Christ-just my opinion on this.) The leaves of the trees are for the healing of the nations. The people will see God's face. (in our human form we cannot look on the face of God and live. Moses was told this when he asked to see God's face). In our glorified, heavenly bodies we will be able to look upon the face of the Lord.

There will be no more death, crying, tears or pain for the former things have passed away.

We will still be able to eat and drink and I doubt we will need weight watchers in heaven! The apostle Paul was taken to heaven and got to see evelything. He said; 'Eye has not seen and ear has not heard the glories that await us in heaven'.

This is the basic details of heaven that are in the Bible. We can speculate about the things that are there and what their purpose may be. I only know that God is not redundant and has a purpose for everything. All of this may reveal other palls of the character of God which he wishes us to know.

What will we do in heaven? Worship and praise the Lord. It doesn't appear that we will need sleep, but we can eat. There will be time to study and learn more of the fullness of the knowledge of the Lord and his creation. We will be able to travel at the speed of thought - which is faster than the speed of light. He may allow us to explore the universe. Look at some of the images from the Hubble Telescope. Awesome. Imagine being able to visit those places just by thinking about being there!

We will know everyone in heaven by name and they will know us. We often think about Bible characters and how fun it will be to speak to Adam, Noah, Daniel or the apostles. But we will also have a chance to visit with historical characters; Washington, Lincoln, and others. We will speak with them as friends and they with us.

I am obviously speculating now! It will be beyond wonder just being in the presence of the Lord. Seeing the nail prints in Jesus hands. Whatever else he has planned for us - count me in.

As you read each chapter keep the end goal in mind, to make an end of sin. I hope this book answers some of your questions and at the least encourages you to be more serious about studying God's word on your own. It is fascinating and fun. You will feel fulfilled and closer to God. You will have more joy and peace in your life and most importantly, you will be ready to respond when Jesus calls us home to be with him

Chapter One

Why would a Loving God allow Evil in the world?

If this question has kept you from making a decision to accept Jesus as Lord and Savior of your life you are not alone. It seems easy for us to accept God as a 'loving God' and we struggle to reconcile that love with all of the evil that surrounds us. If he really is God; all knowing, all powerful, omni-present, etc. then he must have a reason for allowing evil to continue.

We are told by scripture and given the example of Jesus, that God is in essence, 'our Father'. Popular songs have been written about a father's love, our earthly father. But the Bible says that "God's ways are far above our ways". His love is the same; far above our love.

If that's true, then why would such a great love allow his children to experience or to be hurt by the evil that exists in this world? One reason is that this world is temporary and will soon pass away. But the world to come is eternal. In this temporaly world we are learning about the God we will spend eternity with; He wants us to *know* him.

The apostle Paul had two great goals: to spread the plan of salvation to all men - especially his fellow Jews. He even mentioned he would be willing to give up his own salvation if it meant the Jews would then believe and be saved. His second goal was to *know him*. Paul wanted to really know the full character of God, to walk with him and understand him. I think God wants us to understand him as well.

What does it mean to know the full character of someone? How often do we see a news story about a celebrity who has 'fallen'? It may be a politician, sports figure, or even an evangelist. No matter what the situation we are always surprised because the sin/crime/event that creates the fallen state always seems 'out of character'. It seems that way because we only partially knew their character. Their public persona could be drastically different from the one they show in private to friends and family. Friends and family know us 'waits and all'.

Believers in Christ *are* family and fellow heirs to the Father by virtue of our faith in Christ. As family He wants us to know and fully understand Him.

If there were no evil in the world we would only know God's goodness, love, kindness, etc. Without evil there would be nothing harming or threatening to harm us. There would be nothing testing our faith. It would be like Job in the Bible with a protective hedge around us. It may sound comfortable but it is not complete and not nearly as strong a relationship with God as it could be if we had evil pressing around us.

With evil we learn to know God as sanctualy and protector. We also learn what sin is and how God will not *co-exist with sin,* his character is such that he cannot co-exist with sin. This is all the more amazing when we realize that on the cross God allowed Christ (who himself is fully God) to *become sin for us.*

Without sin, we could not know of God's love in all its fullness. We couldn't know of his forbearance, forgiveness, sacrificial love for us, or his plan of salvation for us. Sin and evil allow God to show us the

16

character that only his friends and family would know. A character that he wants all men to know.

The evil in this world that men know and must live with is temporal and finite. The knowledge of God that we learn in this life and in the world to come is eternal and infinite. We have a 'blessed hope' to look forward to entering into one day. A time when there will be no tears, no evil and nothing to impede our relationship with the Lord.

Persecution of the Christian faith has been a part of our history since the beginning of the church. Wherever persecution has been the most severe the faith of the people has become the strongest.

We have been so blessed in America to have freedom of religion. Generations of Christians have been born, matured and died in a country where we were protected and could practice our religion as we saw fit, teach our religion as we saw fit, in a country with many cases decided and legal precedents on the books stating that America is a Christian country. That commitment from the Plymouth settlers to our

Founding Fathers, to our Constitution to the individual statehouses has allowed America to stand up to evil and win.

Twice in the last century America saved the world from itself. A shared faith, a shared purpose and a shared outreach allowed us to be of 'one mind' in a determined effort to defend freedom around the world from tyranny and evil of every type.

Since those victories the Christian faith in America (and the west generally) has become soft. Our church leaders rarely stand up and enter into the public discourse as we have traditionally done. The result of that is our public policy direction no longer looks like the direction that America has historically followed.

Why is this important? When Ben Franklin was asked; 'well Mr. Franklin, what kind of government have you given us?' He replied; 'a Republic Madam if you can keep it.' Why would 'keeping it' be a concern? John Adams said; 'our government was designed for a moral and just people and was wholly inadequate for the governing of any other'. Our Founding Fathers knew the importance of religion and morality in building a society and fairly governing that society. Such a government can't eliminate evil but it can check and control it. Such a government was a gift from God knowing the battles with evil that were ahead and how important it would be to have the tools (laws) necessaly to win that fight. While God allows evil in this world he has given us the means to defeat it spiritually and through the inspired laws of our civil government a means to control it.

The Bible says; 'if you abide in me and my words abide in you, *then* you may receive anything you ask.' God's words did abide in us from the early settlers of America through about 1960. In the early 1960's we took God out of our schools and have been trying to remove him from more and more facets of our lives. Our churches have been brow beaten into believing that the church has no place in the public discourse. Again, if you look at our history you will see that the Church did have a role and played an important part in winning our freedom, writing our founding government documents, having believer's nm for office and win and serve with a humility and sincerity. Is this still happening today? Not nearly as frequently as it should.

While God allows evil to exist, he has given us the means to win in any realm. If we choose to not follow the prescriptions he has given us, we may not win. If you feel the America inspired by God is slipping away then you must know the only fix is a return to serving the Lord. It may be our turn to suffer persecution. How will we respond? Will it make us stronger? The Bible says; 'If *my people* who are called by *my name* will repent and turn from their wicked ways, then I will hear their prayers and heal their land.'

Mankind is not the only part of God'screation that is living with and learning about the meaning of sin and the result of sin. The Bible says that the Angels are watching and long to know the end of these things. Satan was the highest *created* angel. He led approximately one-third of the angels in his rebel- lion against God. The ultimate result of that was the crucifixion of Christ. Imagine being an angel, *knowing* Christ and who he really is and watching that scene unfold. Knowing it was one of their own who began the rebellion. It must have been a horrific scene for them to watch.

But they also can see the beautiful end, how the resurrection gave God the victory and how it paved the way for the salvation of mankind. The peace of mind that they (and we) can now have knowing nothing like this will ever happen again through all eternity to come. Knowing how God said he 'would not let insurrection rise a second time'. There would be no purpose in allowing an insurrection to rise a second time-God has accomplished all he needed. He has shown us his full character and we can spend eternity learning of that character in all its facets with nothing hidden or held back from us.

In summary, God allows evil in this world to:

19

1. Strengthen our faith

2. To show all creation the ultimate result of sin

3. To see His promise to not allow insurrection arise a second time

4. Teaching us about the "blessed hope" of eternity with a loving God

Chapter Two

Why Would a Loving God Create a Hell and Send People There?

Hell was never created for people. It was created for the devil and his angels. God has done everything possible to keep us from going to hell - *including* sending his only Son, Jesus, to take our sins upon himself and die in our place.

How do we know hell is real? Because why would God take the ultimate step of sending his son to die in our place if there was nothing *so awful* to save us from? It is very real. Jesus referenced hell more than once in his teachings and parables; in fact, he referenced hell more than he referenced heaven.

The Bible says the wages of sin is death. ALL sin is a capital offense, there are no plea bargains al- lowed. God cannot live with sin. We are all sinners and we have all sinned. The ONLY way out and the only PERMANENT solution to sin is Christ crucified and faith in his work on the cross for us.

I attended a church years ago where the pastor and elder believed a 'loving God would never create and/or send anyone to hell'. God is love. Hell is really just a separation from God. There are many folks who today would fall in this category. But if a sinner (who already has separated himself from God - via his sin) dies and his punishment is 'separation from God', what has changed for him? He wouldn't care about being separated from God, he has shown that in how he lived his life and in his refusal to accept Christ's salvation for his life. Does that sound like justice to you?

Of course not. The Bible tells us that someday every knee will bow and acknowledge Jesus as Lord and Savior and his judgements as just and true. Love without judgement is not justice.

Unfortunately, today we somehow feel we have 'moved beyond ' such measures. We act as Job's friends in the Old Testament, in essence, saying we trust our feelings and our measure of justice more than we trust God. Basically, we are setting ourselves up as God.

There are a lot of things that are not preached from the pulpit today-and should be taught because they can change our ultimate salvation and destiny and change how we live in this life. Preachers have an obligation to 'preach the word in season and out'; to 'preach the faith once delivered to the saints'. God didn't have any rewrites and revisions in his word. He gave it to us as he wanted us to have it. In fact, there are warnings in the Bible for those who would change as much as a 'dot and tittle '. To add or subtract from his word is a punishable offense. But we do that evelyday in our 'modem age'.

The result of that is a watered down gospel. Churches are pursuing growth in the numbers of their members with little regard to the spiritual growth of their members. Churches fear losing financial support and so there are topics that are taboo. One of the main taboo subjects is hell. If you are not certain of your salvation then hell is most definitely an uncomfortable topic. If you are celtain of your salvation then hell is a topic that should spur youon to be more effective in your wit- ness to others. God is not willing that any should perish but that ALL come to repentance in Christ. Our witness should follow his desire. Our witness should be ongoing, diligent and reflected in our lives. No one wants a family member or dear friend to go to hell. We should feel that same sentiment for every person in the world. We don't have to hit others over the head with the gospel everyday. But we also shouldn't ignore the issue when it comes up naturally in conversation and life. Those opportunities are God at work. He wants us to share when he puts us in that position. Let's not let him down.

Some would say, ok, but does hell have to be eternal? Salvation is eternal, eternity is God's natural state. The present world as we know it and the time that is a part of it, is temporal. We often see in scripture a reference to 'the appointed time'. After the Thousand year reign of Christ on this earth, there is no reference to time because in an eternal environment time simply has no meaning.

Every child born in this world is an eternal being. Our spirit will never die. That cannot be changed. So the places where we will spend our future; either heaven or hell, by necessity also have to be eternal.

Are there degrees of punishment in hell? It seems it is easier for us to accept a hell if there are in fact degrees of punishment in hell. Jesus made it plain that failing the Ten Commandments on just one point was enough to send someone to hell. In some cases just thinking a sin would be enough to convict us of that sin. He was saying it is impossible for us to 'make the grade' on our own efforts.

We view murderers as being worse sinners than liars and therefore accept a harsher punishment for them. It seems this is the human way to look at it. A Hitler should suffer a harsher sentence than an adulterer. If there are degrees of punishment in Hell I believe that is above my pay grade. But I am completely comfortable in trusting God to handle all of that in a way that is just and fair.

The Christian religion is the only religion that says we cannot work our way to heaven. Every other religion says that in one way or form, via works in this life or in reincarnated states we can continue working until we get to heaven or become some sort of God ourselves.

The Bible is vely clear. There is one mediator between God and man, Jesus Christ. He is our only hope of salvation and in Him we can be certain of our salvation. We can be celtain that we will never have to experience hell.

The Bible says there are no tears in Heaven. If we get there and we have loved ones who are not there, how can we not have tears and be distraught over their situation? We will have a more full knowledge of God when we get to heaven. There is also a curious passage that talks of 'the books being open'. In this passage it evidently is not having the books opened for judgement but for our information. This will be during the thousand year reign of Christ.

If this allows us to follow the lives of loved ones who are not there, we will be able to see the many, many, many chances where God placed the plan of salvation in their path. We will see how time and again they either said no outright or put their decision off for 'later'. It will be difficult to see this but over the course of a thousand years we will be able to accept it. We will be able to bow our knees to the Lord and acknowledge that his judgements are just and true. We will be able to do that with no bitterness because we will see the power of God's love in their lives. We will be able to see the depth of his love for them and how often he tried to draw them unto himself. We will see how God was always with them and never against them. Over a thousand year period we will be at peace with God's dealings with all people and we will be able to enter into eternity with no doubts. If your church does not talk of hell then you will need to get in the scriptures and read about it for your- self. This will help you understand the depth of God's love in offering Jesus to die on the cross for you. He never wanted you or anyone else to go to hell.

Unfortunately, many folks make the decision to do just that. God, who gave us free will, does not interfere. If we choose not to accept his path he will allow us to suffer the consequences. So... choose LIFE, choose Christ.

Chapter Three

Why Would a Loving God Allow Men to choose which Books should be included in the Bible?

The issue here is how can we know that we can trust the validity of scripture, how can we know that the Bible as we know it is in fact God's word-revealed to us in the way he wanted us to have it?

I had a conversation years ago with my older brother who in essence was questioning the accuracy of the Bible because of the many years and generations in which it was passed on verbally before it was ever written down.

That got me thinking of a way to illustrate that history that would be easy to understand. I came up with a bar chart showing the lives of each of the Old Testament heroes and how their lives overlapped. It was fascinating and I have included it here for you. You can see that Noah's father could have known Adam. They could have talked directly.

If our father tells us of something he has experienced in his life we know we can believe them. Just as Noah knew he could believe his father and trust what he was telling him was true. The stories that were probably passed on generation by generation by generation ... could have also been passed on directly from those who were involved in the story. This got the stories to the point where they were written down and eliminated the many middlemen so to speak.

I have even thought how many fathers may have taken their sons when they reached maturity to journey and go to meet Adam directly. To sit and listen to him retell the events of his life. How he walked with God in the Garden of Eden. How he felt when he first saw Eve. How he named the animals and how tending God's garden did not seem like work. How he wilfully sinned and brought sin into the world. Would that make an impression on a young boy? I think it would make a lifelong impression.

Look at the chart. See how those lives overlapped and how each of those could have told many generations directly about the events of their lives. This would make the accuracy of the written testimony to be much more accurate than it could have been othe1wise even without the guidance of the Lord.

The Bible says that all scripture is given by the Holy Spirit. When the writers began writing down the stories they were told or the stories they experienced, God was with them. God was the author.

I read a story about a man who had a company with a computer program that could tell if a book was written by the same person or not. He was called as an expert witness in many trials where plagiarism was an issue. He was extremely successful. He was also an unbeliever and having had such success he decided he would feed the Bible into his computer and prove the Bible was written by men only - and therefore subject to error and confusion.

The Bible as we know it was written over a period of about 1,400-1,500 years. It was written by over 40 authors in three different languages. He thought this would be a slam dunk for his computer to refute. After many weeks of data entry he fed it into his computer program and awaited the results. Many, many hours later the computer printed out its results and it said: 'one author'. He refused to believe it and trusting his own work, i.e., his computer, he re-ran the analysis. The answer once again said; one author. This man trusted his computer completely and as a result became a Christian.

To this man, he had the 'proof he needed to become a believer. He had spent many years and many dollars perfecting his software system to analyze the written word. His program was trusted enough that the court allowed him to use his program and be an expert witness in many court cases.

Most of us don't have that sort of secular confirmation. We have to take God's word by faith. I think that's the way God wants it.

OK, even if that is true, there were many books that were not included when our Bible was compiled. The decision on whether or not a particular book was 'scripture ' or not, was left to men. Men make mistakes. My brother thought this proved his point.

The proof is once again, faith. Do you think God would inspire all of these writers and then leave it to chance to see what they do with it? God is involved from start to finish. From the inspiration of the original writing, to the assembly of the Bible. To the preaching and teaching and reading of the Bible to its practical application in our daily life.

One third of the Bible was prophetic at the time it was written. Many of those prophecies have come true. Fulfilled prophecy is the best proof we have to the validity of scripture. No other text for any religion can boast fulfilled prophecy like the Bible. Fulfilled prophecy is so accurate that many sceptics think it must have been written after the fact. They simply cannot believe anyone (even God) could foretell the future so accurately.

When copying the Bible ancient scribes were not allowed to erase or make corrections of any kind. Each copy had to be perfect. If a mistake was made that page had to be burned and a new page done to replace it.

God took great care to give us his word knowing it would be used by man on earth until the second coming of Christ. I think it will also be used in Heaven as a teaching tool for eternity. God has revealed himself in his word and wants us to know him. His written word will do just that.

In summary, his word was shared verbally for many years to other generations by the people who were a part of the story. They shared their history and God allowed them to accurately remember the stories and comments He wished to be passed to future generations. The long lives they lived in those early days allowed them to speak directly to many future generations without any middlemen who could make mistakes in the re-telling.

God inspired the authors as they wrote these stories down. He also inspired the men who were in charge of compiling these individual books into the compilation we know today as the Bible. He then inspires us as we read and study the Bible today. God has been in full control and authority of his word from the initial experiences in the lives of the people who experienced the stories, to the writing, compilation and distribution of his word to those of us who today read and study his word. We can read his word with confidence knowing 'his word will not come back to him void but will accomplish the purpose for which he sent it'.

There is a saying from generations ago which sounds right today. A faith in his word that is mocked today, but one we would do well to consider and remember; 'God said it, I believe it, and that ends it'.

Chapter Four

Why Would a Loving God Leave it to Men to Share His Plan of Salvation?

This may be the most important topic in this book. Salvation is everything. Salvation is our graduation to the eternal world with God. Salvation is a free gift. It has been bought and paid for by Jesus with his sacrificial death on the cross and more importantly, his resurrection which proves his authority to act on our behalf and be our substitute.

We must only believe it and accept it. To me, this is a no brainer. No one in their right mind could refuse this. The hard palt is living with Jesus as Lord and Savior after we have accepted him. That requires us to submit our will to His on a daily basis. That requires us to put our pride away and humble our- selves to Him.

In an earlier chapter we showed how we can trust God's word. How it is trustworthy and how His word will accomplish his purpose. When we say he leaves it to man to share the plan of salvation, he doesn't leave us alone. He gives us his Word and he gives us his Spirit to help us accomplish our and His purpose.

The Bible tells us that at the time that we accept Christ as Lord and Savior he gives each of us 'a measure of faith'. I have found over the years in my Bible study that the Lord is very specific and He is never redundant. He says what He means and He means what He says.

In the case above, He gives us a measure of faith; not the measure of faith. 'A' measure can be different for everyone. 'The' measure would be the same for evelyone.

He gives us 'a different' measure because he has given each of us a different purpose in the corporate church whose mission it is to save souls. The apostle Paul talks about that; some teachers, some have the gift of prophecy, some healers, some helpers, some speak in tongues, etc. He compares it to palts of the body; all are not a hand or a foot. But all are needed and none more important than the others. The Bible says that the Spirit gives gifts as He sees fit; he gives them liberally as he sees fit. He knows our mission and will equip us to accomplish his mission.

I am sure that some folks know the instant they are saved what their mission is to be in the body of Christ. For most, it requires us to pray, study his Word, mature in our faith until God knows we are ready. At that point our mission will be apparent to us or God will communicate that to us.

People who say that God leaves the plan of salvation for man to share with others just don't know the whole story. Man may be used to spearhead the effort but He is with us in His Word and in His Spirit. We are definitely not alone!

The Apostles were hiding in their room after the crucifixion, they were afraid. When the Holy Spirit descended on them they were changed men and spoke boldly for the cause of Christ. Some who knew them even questioned if these were the same men! That same Spirit indwells us from the point where we first believed. We too are not alone. God says His Spilit will bring all things to remembrance to us. We can be bold knowing we have his Word and his Spirit to help us. Reach out to those you know who need Christ and to all you may meet that may need him also. You may be acting specifically

on a mission for God in doing so.

The Apostles were men like us. The Spirit transformed them just the same way he can transform us. We have a weapon that they lacked ... we have God's written word in the form of the New Testament to add to the written word in the Old Testament. It has been said that the Old Testament is the New Testament concealed. And that the New Testament is the Old Testament revealed. We have in written f01m a more complete knowledge of the Lord than they had.

God's word is not just a book like Gone With the Wind. God's word is alive in its purpose and in its caretaking of us. How often have you read the Bible and after rereading a familiar passage you find yourself saying; 'I've never seen that before '. The Spirit of the Lord will emphasize specific nuances in his word that we need - when we need it. God's word can be read and studied on more than one level. This is how he can give us exactly what we need at the moment we need it.

The Apostles wrote what they experienced and we have that with us today. We also have experiences. While that can be good it can also mislead us. Today it may be because of the influences of eastern and other esoteric religions, the Politically Correct police or liberal courts that can influence many folks to the point of being spiritually confused. We are told that if anything contradicts the Bible and the Lordship of Christ that we should ignore it. Sadly, many today put the authority of their experiences over scripture. That path is one that will lead to complete confusion.

We have his Spirit who can embolden us and bring all (scriptural) things to remembrance. We have his Word which contains most all of the full counsel of God. We have the desire in our healt that God placed in us when we became believers. God's Word is our ultimate authority. He tells us in his Word to 'test the spirits'. How? Test them against his Word. If there is no contradiction, no problem.

You can also test your experiences against God's Word. Was your experience one that would lead you away from or to Christ? Any experience that confilms Jesus as Lord and Savior will pass muster.

Our experiences are given to us specifically. People tend to trust the counsel of those who have 'gone through the same things I am going through now'. Right or wrong we tend to do so. EVEN SO, the advice and counsel we get from anyone should be weighed against scripture. If the counsel is of God it will not contradict His Word and it will be directly helpful to you at that particular moment in your life.

Many folks who are well meaning can also be misguided. They may say in all earnestness; 'I have a word from the Lord for you'. Try not to be confrontational and tell them you will test their word against God's Word . If it agrees you may accept it or ask God for confirmation. Remember, if it is of God the word they share will never contradict scripture.

Finally, I think God allows men to be the stewards of His Word because we too are 'sinners saved by grace '. We have been in the shoes of those to whom we have shared the gospel. Our witness is a positive motivator for folks trying to make a decision for Christ. Our witness takes the gospel out of the pages of the Bible and places it into contemporaly life. If it changed us, it can change them also.

Chapter Five

Why Would a Loving God Delay His Return?

We sometimes assume that the Lord's return has been delayed. If it has been delayed there are good reasons for it. I rather think that His return is right on schedule. Ecclesiastes states there is a time for eve1ything; to be born, to die, to sew and reap, a time for love and a time for hate, etc.

If the Bible tells us there is a specific time for these small things, then how much more so for the greatest thing of all; the return of Jesus as Lord to and for this world.

The return of Christ can actually be looked at as two different events. The first event is the Rapture in which He will appear to meet all believers worldwide who are 'caught up ' to meet Him and to be escorted back to Heaven by Him. This event will change everything for everyone. For those caught up to meet Him, it will mark the start of our eternal relationship with Christ. For those left behind on earth, it will mark the beginning of a rapid slide into the abyss of rampant evil running wild. The Bible says that God is not willing that any should perish but that all should be brought to salvation. After the Rapture there will be a great increase of evil from man against man. It will mark a seven year period during which the antichrist will ascend to a position of world-wide leadership.

Towards the end of that seven year period mankind will experience the judgment of God against man. It will be severe, so much so that men's hea1is will fail them for fear - some will literally be scared to death.

Going back to Ecclesiastes, there will be a point in time when God knows that there is no one else on earth who will change their heart and accept the Gospel of Jesus. That's the point when the Return will occur. So if God is delaying, He is simply waiting to get to that point where evelyone who will accept Him has in fact, accepted Him. We don't know when that will be but we know it could be at any time.

Are you ready? Which side of the line would you fall on if Jesus returned today? It is not too late, you can accept Jesus as Lord and Savior of your life today ... right now. Sincerely say this prayer:

"Lord, forgive me of my sin. Forgive me for my hard headedness and refusing to tum to you until now. I accept Jesus as Lord and Savior of my life. I accept his sacrifice on the cross as payments for my sins. Please send your Spirit to dwell in and guide me from this point forward. I accept you as Lord of my life. Thank you, in Jesus name, Amen."

Find a church that teaches scripture. Study with one of the teachers or elders and as soon as you can get baptized in the name of the Father, Son and Holy Spirit. Baptism isn't a requirement for salvation but it should be one of the first acts of obedience by a new believer. It is symbolic of your being born again into a new life with Jesus. It is also a public profession of your faith in Christ. In scripture Jesus said; "If you acknowledge me before men I will acknowledge you before the Father".

The folks left on this world after the Rapture will have a hell on ealih to live through prior to the actual second coming of Jesus to this world. What will those who have been raptured be doing during this time? They will be attending the 'wedding supper of the Lamb" as described in scripture. Prior to His ascension Jesus told his disciples he would 'not drink wine again until the marriage supper of the Lamb '. The marriage supper symbolism is used because Jesus likened the church as his bride.

It will be a celebration unlike any we have ever seen. In addition to a heavenly buffet, I believe this is where we will each get our 'rewards' in a 'Believer's Judgment'. The Bible says there is 'now no condemnation for them that are in Christ Jesus'. The rewards we receive will be crowns representing many things; faith, salvation, soul winners, looking for the appearance of Christ, etc. The Bible says we will throw our crowns at Jesus' feet as a form of worship. While we will all be thankful to be saved, we should all also wish to have at least one crown to offer Him in worship.

These crowns will be worn for eternity and will act like rankings in the military. People will know what we did in this life by the crowns we wear. This will not promote jealousy and envy, they will simply reflect the honor deserved as a faithful believer.

Jesus has also been preparing a place for us; our own living quarters for eternity. I believe we will each be shown our new home during this initial seven year period. I am sure it will be beyond our imagining. The Apostle Paul (who was transported to and saw the third heaven) said 'eye has not seen and ear has not heard the glories that await us'.

For those of us caught up to Heaven this will be a time of unparalleled joy, excitement, and thankful- ness. Quite a contrast to those left behind on earth. For those of us caught up in the rapture, we will be the only generation that will not have to experience a physical death. If you have ever watched a loved one die then you know how most suffer a great deal as they die. Skipping this process is a special blessing for all of us.

The Bible says that Jesus is not slack concerning his promise; i.e., delaying his coming again. He is merely awaiting the appointed time. Only the Father knows that appointed time. The closest we can get is to know the general season. Jesus chastised the Jewish leaders of his day because they did not recognize the signs of the times. He expected them to know the season. If he expected them to know the season of his first appearance, then it is only reasonable to assume he will expect us to know the season of his second coming.

That season is upon us, we are the generation of his coming. We can't know the day but we can know the season. We will look at this in more detail in a future chapter. The appointed time will soon be upon us.

Chapter Six

Eve Was Deceived but Adam Wilfully Sinned

Outside of the stories of creation and the flood, this may be the most famous of the Old Testament stories. As a child, when I heard this story I had the opinion that after Eve ate the fruit she went running through the Garden to find Adam and share the fruit with him.

However, if you read the story you will see that Eve gave the fruit to the man who was with her. Adam was standing right beside Eve. He watched the serpent tempt her. He watched her deception and watched as she ate the fruit. Adam knew it was wrong and could have stopped her - but he did not.

The Bible says that Eve was deceived when she ate the fruit so it was not imputed to her as sin. Adam willfully took the fruit and ate, that's why his action was imputed to him as sin. That is why 'sin entered the world through Adam'.

Until this point, in all of creation including the Angels, there was no knowledge of and description of Sin. Much less, the results of sin and its actions upon men and creation.

God gave man free will just as he gave the Angels free will. He does not want us worshipping Him out of fear, He wants our worship freely given. If God immediately killed any Angel who sinned, what kind of worship do you think he would receive? Fear would permeate all of the Angelic ranks, they would be afraid that any action of theirs could at any time be called sin and then they too would have to suffer a death penalty. This does not describe a healthy environment does it?

Even though one third of the Angels followed Satan in his rebellion, God chose not to immediately execute them. He thought it best to let sin play out, to let all of creation see the awful results of sin and how God's direction to not sin is more than a simple direction, it is an imperative for a better creation and a more joyous life for all creation. In essence, this creation where time is so important is a dress rehearsal for the eternity to come. Sin will play out fully, it has already been defeated, judgment will be carried out and then eternity will begin where there is no sin and never will be sin again. God says he will not let insurrection rise a second time.

What did sin do in this world? It entered through Adam and is passed through generations from father to the children. There are at least three references in the Bible about the 'sins of the father being passed to the 3rd generation '. Also, how the blessings of the father are passed to the thousandth generation, i.e., forever.

I believe the prayer of a parent for a child may be the most powerful prayer we can offer. God has the children in a special place. Jesus warned of the punishment for anyone who hurt one of his children. One of my prayers has been; 'to let any generational curse end with me and NOT be passed along to my son. Lord, give him a fresh stalt and teach him to walk with you. 'I believe that is a prayer that God will honor. There is enough sin in the world, enough problems our children will face and have to overcome, let them enter into those battles without the luggage of the sins of prior generations.

Women have a sin nature also, but they cannot pass it on to their children, that is done through the man. That is how Jesus could have been born of a human mother and not have a sin nature. His father was the Holy Spirit.

Mary, the mother of Jesus, was blessed among all women, but she was not sinless. She was a human being with a sin nature like all of us. She could not pass that sin nature along. When you understand this you can see that Mary was not divine, she didn't have to be. She was blessed among women and accepted the word of the Lord concerning her pregnancy and her son who was destined to be the Savior.

What if the Adam and Eve story was reversed? What if Adam was deceived and Eve was the one who willfully sinned? That would have been a problem. If the sin nature was passed along by the mother, then the Savior could not have been born fully God and fully human, without a sin nature. God knew exactly what He was doing. He provided a Savior for mankind in the only way it could have been done. Thank you Lord.

Chapter Seven

Why Would a Loving God tell Israel to kill All men, women and children in certain Villages?

These stories have troubled many, many people over the years. We know our God is a loving God. We know how He wishes us to protect life at all costs. These stories just seems so inconsistent with His character as we know it.

Some people when learning of these stories begin to think of God as a mean judge, like Zeus sitting on his throne eagerly throwing lightning bolts to the earth destroying people. Nothing could be further from the truth.

What if I told you that instead of these st01ies showing the anger of God that they in fact show His love? When you understand the full story you will agree.

Many years ago as a young Christian I hosted a neighborhood get together to discuss prophecy and the Lord's return. One of the ladies there brought up these stories of God telling the Israelites to destroy everyone in these villages. She didn't understand it and it troubled her. I did not know the full story and could not answer her except for platitudes. I vowed to be better prepared in the future.

At the same time I had my own story that troubled me, I just didn't understand it. There are fallen Angels who have been in chains in Hell for thousands of years. God is not allowing them full movement, any movement. Yet their ring leader, Satan, is allowed to move freely throughout creation and to accuse us before the throne day and night. It made no sense to me.

Imagine my surprise when I found out that the story that troubled me was in fact linked to the story that troubled her. It starts in the 6th chapter of Genesis where it describes the 'sons of God (fallen Angels) having relations with the daughters of men. Their offspring in many cases were giants. There are fossil records showing bones of 'humans' that were eight to twelve feet tall.

The fallen Angels who engaged in this activity are the Angels in chains, in Hell. Their Satanic plan was to so pollute the human DNA that there would not be a pure line from which the Savior could be born. If they had been successful you and I would have no hope of salvation. It was an insidious plan that God wanted crushed out.

There is a description of Noah that I also have wondered about. I thought it was a way of saying how 'good' Noah was. In light of our conversation here, you can see how once again the Bible is so specific saying just what God wants to say and Him meaning everything He says. It describes Noah as a man who was 'pelfect in His generations'. The line of Noah had not yet been infected by any demonic DNA. After the flood, stalting over with Noah and his family would give mankind a fresh and pure start.

This same problem happened again after the flood in a much smaller way and God told the Israelites to take care of it. These are the villages in question. These villages had a con11pt DNA and had to be wiped out so they could not spread that infection to other humans. God did not do this gleefully, I'm sure He had a heavy healt. But the sacrifice of a few thousand long ago insured the salvation of Billions to come. This was not an act of anger, it was an act of love for all of mankind.

Chapter Eight

Why Would a Loving God Choose
Israel to be His People?

The Bible says that God chose Israel to be His people because of the 'faith of the patriarchs'. Abraham, Isaac and Jacob.

Remember how in an earlier chapter we looked at generational curses? How they can flow to the 3rd generation? We also mentioned how the blessings can flow to the thousandth generation. The Patriarchs are an example of that. The whole world has been blessed through the faith of the patriarchs. The Jews have been a beacon to us all. They are the 'elect' of God the Father.

The Savior of the world, Jesus, was a Jew. The authors of the Bible for the most part have all been Jews. The Apostle Paul who wrote most of the New Testament was a Jew. Many scientific advancements over the years have come from Jewish scientists. Through the Jew the whole world has been blessed many times over.

Can one man effect a change that will alter the history of mankind? Abraham did. Are the Jews 'better ' than other nationalities? Were they better in the past? Of course not, but they were faithful and that honored God. One of the things to me that proves that the Bible is God's word is the fact that He never sugar-coats the individuals that we know from their stories in the Bible. He tells us all about them, waits and all. They were men, they had failings as well as successes. They are held up to us not because they are perfect, but because they were faithful.

Their complete histories can be used as an example or as a crutch. I have heard many men over the years talk about David's adultely and how God said that 'David is a man after my own heart '. It is very, very dangerous to use a failing of David's as an allowance for ours. Yes, we fail and sin. Yes, God knows that. But He expects us to continue to work out our salvation and become more and more Christ like in our walk with Him. He doesn't want us to hide behind an Old Testament story to cover our sin. Jesus covers our sins, there is no other substitute for the work of Christ. The Bible says there is One God and One Mediator between God and man, Christ Jesus.

Yes, there was much in David's life for us to emulate. Look also at Daniel and Joseph. Similar in that they were imprisoned for years before God chose to use them. During all that time when it seemed they had been forgotten they never lost their faith. In fact, their faith never wavered. Could you have a similar resolve? Could your trust in the Lord never even waver? Study the 11th Chapter of Hebrews that is the Hall of Fame of Faith. Their stories were meant to inspire us in our daily life.

I have stated that Israel is the 'elect' of God the Father, they are His chosen people. The Church is the 'elect' of God the Son, Christ. When you study the Bible you must be sure of which group of 'elect' is being discussed or you will be greatly confused.

Salvation was given to the Jews first. Through them it was given to all men. The 'elect' of the Father shared salvation with all mankind through the Church; the 'elect' of God the Son. We have much to thank them for.

Chapter Nine

Why Would a Loving God send His Only Son to Save Us? Surely there must have been another way

The Bible says that 'without the shedding of blood there is no forgiveness of sin'. For many people today this seems so harsh. Capital punishment. Capital punishment is a hot button that is still the subject of debate whenever a State prepares to carry out the death penalty on a prisoner. It never ceases to amaze me how the opponents of Capital Punishment are usually the most staunch supporter s of abortion!

The Bible does describe Capital Punishment. When our judicial process completes its course and a person is 'judged' guilty of a capital offense, then the sentence can be carried out by the State without guilt. Opponents will argue how there have been cases where 'innocent' people have been executed and we should abolish capital punishment to keep that from ever happening again.

Have there been such cases? I don't know for sure but I know I cannot state conclusively that no innocent person has ever been executed. I can state conclusively that every aborted baby is innocent. More than 50 million since Roe vs. Wade was decided.

I can also state conclusively that every person who has ever lived, man or woman, was a sinner and by God's measure deserving of death. This just cannot be debated. The Bible says; 'all have sinned and fallen short of the glory of God '.

We have a problem with capital punishment, the shedding of blood. It seems so antiquated. The Bible says that 'God is the same yesterday, today and forever '. We also have a problem understanding the purity of God; how God cannot co-exist with sin. We co-exist with sin eve1yday. Many of us feel we are 'good people '. In the Bible God says 'My ways are not your ways. My ways are above your ways '. In fact, His ways are so far above our ways that we really cannot comprehend the difference.

We know the Bible story how sin entered the world through Adam. How they were not embarrassed about their nakedness until after their sin. How God clothed them with animal skins and this was in essence the first sacrifice. The shedding of blood that gave them forgiveness for their sin.

Animal sacrifice was one of the basic tenants of the Jewish religion. Passover, rubbing lamb's blood on the posts and lentils of their doorway in Egypt spared them from the death angel. Blood was the basis of life to the ancient Israelites. We can argue today about death, brain death, etc. But we cannot argue that without blood there is no life.

It is interesting that with blood being so revered as a part of life, they could not eat meat unless it had been fully drained of blood. Meat that is not fully drained spoils quickly. When we speak of humanity today it is not unusual to hear someone use the phrase flesh and blood. When Christ appeared to the Apostles he asked them to touch him and see that He is not a ghost. He said; 'Does a ghost have flesh and bone like you see that I have?' In His glorified form he had flesh and bone, but evidently no blood. Our glorified body will be like His. We will recognize each other by sight. We will look much like we do today. The exception? Somehow our glorified body's physiology will be changed to allow us to live without blood.

Let's go back and look at the shedding of blood for the forgiveness of sin. Animal sacrifice and its atonement for sin was temporary and had to be done again and again as a part of their worship. If a lesser created being (animal, bird, etc.) can be a temporary atonement for a greater created being (man), then the converse is a higher beings sacrifice for a lower being would be pe1manent.

If that is true, then an Angelic sacrifice for man would be pe1manent. A higher Angelic sac1ifice would undo that requiring a higher Angelic sac1ifice to win it back, etc. This would culminate in Jesus Him- self, offering Himself, as a pe1manent sacrifice for all of humanity.

Sort of like boys playing a pickup game of baseball. In seeing who gets to bat first they toss a bat between them then hand over hand work their way to the top to see who is the last hand that can hold the bat. That team will bat first.

Jesus was always the 'top hand'. He came to offer himself knowing there was nothing the 'other side' could ever do to overcome His sacrifice. Anyone on His team is a part of the 'winning team'. There was no point in having all of these inte1mediate sacrifices because ultimately, Jesus had already volunteered to be our sacrifice from before the foundation of the world.

Sin did not take God by surprise. He knew it would come and He knew it was necessa1y to teach all of creation about the full character of God, the full ravages of sin and how creation is enhanced without sin.

Jesus was the only permanent solution to sin. A sacrifice once and for all time. Thank you Lord.

When Mary was at the tomb and recognized Jesus she automatically went to hug him. He said 'do not touch me for I have not yet ascended to my Father and been glorified '. About a week later he told His disciples to touch him and see that He was not a ghost. Obviously, He had ascended to His Father and been glorified between these two appearances.

We are not told specifically what it meant for Jesus to be glorified so we will have to speculate. This is just MY OPINION. Moses was told to make the altar in the tabernacle on the 'pattern of the altar in Heaven'.

Moses basically made a copy. The original altar was and still is in heaven. It is easy to imagine it being somewhere near God's throne to act as a constant reminder of God's mercy to us (which we don't deserve).

The Second Coming of Jesus to earth will be in two phases; the Rapture and then His actual coming to the earth. I imagine his ascension in the same way. He first ascends to be glorified then returns to paradise to lead all those souls to heaven in the great Resurrection.

When He is glorified, He comes alone as a conquering King who has defeated death, sin and Satan. He approaches the altar (just MY OPINION here) and in some manner sheds HIS blood on the altar. It would only have to be one drop of His holy blood to act as a sacrifice. It could be an angel bringing a cup or bowl of Jesus' blood from the cross. However it is done, Jesus will return to the glory of his natural appearance. His resurrected body will morph into the 'fully God' body that John sees in the Book of Revelation, the God of

Judgment. This is His body in the spiritual realm. When He returns to earth and to paradise, he will take on His earthly body - the one that is familiar to all who have known Him. This is the body that He uses during all of the post resurrection appearances on earth. It is a sort of hybrid body. It appears to be fully human but He has the abilities of His spiritual body; i.e. walking on water, going through walls and doors, appearing and disappearing, etc.

Jesus did this for a couple of reasons. First, He wanted to be recognized. He wanted the people to know that He did in fact rise from the dead and is now living again. I also believe that He knew that people were not yet ready to see Him in His full glorified state. Most would probably have hidden in fear rather than face the God of the universe in His natural state. God told Moses he could not see the face of God and live. We can assume that restriction would still be in force and that humans are not capable of looking on the face of the Lord and live, we just cannot survive that possibility in our human form.

I can imagine the silence in heaven as Jesus approached the altar. Once His blood is poured or dropped on the alter I can imagine God saying once again; 'this is my beloved Son in whom I am well pleased ' and then ALL of heaven breaks out in song and praise to Jesus, God the Son, who will forever be known as 'King of Kings and Lord of Lords '!

At this point, the 'work of Christ' is done, all has been accomplished. The ramifications of His life's work are still reverberating to this day, and will continue to do so for all eternity.

We have known Jesus as Lord and Savior. On His return, all will know Him as Lord and Judge. Yes, it will be

Christ who judges every man and woman. After that judgment every knee will bow and acknowledge Jesus as Lord and His judgments as just and true. No one will be able to complain that they didn't get a fair shake.

We should all hope that we can hear Him say to us on that day: 'well done thou good and faithful servant '.

Chapter Ten

Why Would a Loving God Take so Long To Create the World?

In the Bible God says; 'I will confound the wisdom of the wise'. In the few places in the Bible where it talks about God laughing, in evely case He is laughing at the folly of man. We think we are so smart. We have an accumulated body of knowledge now that is larger and easier to access that at any time in the history of mankind; we think that makes us smart.

I think if we could test Adam's brain he would test off our chalts. Men have always been smalt, they just have not always had the tools to recall information like we can in our age.

There have always been skeptics about the creation story in the Bible. In days of old the skeptics treated the believers with deference and courtesy. It was not until the Scopes Trial in the early part of the last century that the media began to speak of believers with contempt and derision. It became o.k. to make fun of us who believed the Bible as the infallible word of God. That has continued to this day and has become much worse. Unfortunately, it seems many in the church fear the derision of men more than the consequences of not speaking boldly for the Lord; we need to overcome that.

The scopes trial was about the teaching of evolution in Tennessee public schools. At that time only creation was taught in Tennessee schools. A teacher who offered evolution was on trial. The lawyer for the prosecution was a famous preacher (William Jennings Bryan) who twice was a candidate for President of the United States.

During the trial he took the stand and was tripped up by the defense attorney (Clarence Darrow) into saying that a 'day' in the creation story 'could have been' longer than a twenty four hour period. Once you cross that threshold you have opened the door to all kinds of doubt and alternatives for what is actually written in the Bible. I believe at the time that Mr. Bryan was suffering heart problems and other ailments that kept him from being his best. He died just days after the trial.

My take on creation always comes from the other side, I turn it upside down. If God is truly God and all powerful, then He could have created everything in an instant just with a spoken word. When I study the creation story my question is 'why did God take so long to create the world?' There must have been a reason.

Before creation there was 'eternity past '. After the judgment of the Lord there will be 'eternity future '. In both cases time will have no meaning. We live in a physical, created environment and time is critically important. So God was not just creating our physical world, he was creating and teaching us about time. He taught us how to measure it. The evening and the morning were the first day, the second day, etc. Six days you will work and on the seventh (Sabbath day) you will rest. The moon is how we measure months. Years were a total of twelve months, etc. God said the 'sun, moon and stars were to measure the days, months and years '.

Going back to the Scopes trial; was a 'day' always a 24hour day? The word used in Genesis for 'day' is the same word used for 'Sabbath', which as we know has always been a 24 hour day. Yes, those are all 24 hour days. Six 24 hour days of creation and one 24 hour day of rest.

The Bible also says that at the end of His creation God looked at all that he had made and said that it was good. God didn't make a primordial stew where he had to wait eons to see how it would turn out and whether in fact it would be good.

God created a fully grown, fully mature world. How old was Adam when God made him? We don't know whether he had the characteristics of a man of 15, 25, 35, 55, etc. What we do know is that Adam was fully grown and fully mature. That is the way He made all of creation. The mountains were fully formed, the liver gorges were already cut, the grasses were grown, the cattle and other animals were adults, etc. All of creation had the characteristics of age even though they were brand new.

This means that rocks, fossils, fauna, etc. all had the characteristics of age even though they were also brand new. Remember how God said He would confound the wisdom of the wise? This is one way He does so. He wants us to accept Him and His creation by faith. He wants us to accept His salvation by faith. That's why I don't think we will ever find Noah's ark that would be a proof of the truth of scripture and would bypass the need for faith.

I have been ridiculed for this position in the media. Some folks are simply so hardened in their heart that they cannot even consider another potential explanation. They celtainly can't argue it. When they can't argue a point the only thing they have left is to belittle the one making the point. Jesus said count it a blessing when you have been ridiculed because of my name.

God is either the God of the universe or He is not. If He is, if He created all things in His way in His time, then we would do well to study our history in light of that fact.

Creation gives value to us individually. We are made in the image of God. We are unique and special.

Evolution says we are an accident and of no special value. Which view would give our children a higher estimation of themselves and others? Which teaches the tremendous value and importance of life?

Life is simply better with a belief in and a knowledge of the Lord of Life, God Almighty. When life has a value of its own society becomes more refined and more spiritually focused.

A belief in creation explains all of this. God loves humanity but God loves us individually also. We have value to the Lord of the Universe. We have a purpose in this life, we are not an accident. We should therefore value each other.

Chapter Eleven

Is the Bible Really God's Word? Inspired and Without Error?

The Bible has sold more copies around the world than any other book that has ever been published. It is not even close, second place on the list is so far behind that we don't even know which book should be placed there.

There are many inspirational books that have been printed over the years. Some dealing with faith, some dealing with personal improvement and 'self-help'. Any book that has a positive effect on the reader that causes him/her to be more positive with other folks is always welcome. But no other book has the transformational qualities of the Bible.

People suffering from addiction have choices of many '10 step' type programs and some do in fact make a change at least temporarily. But many relapse into their bad habits of the past. When you look for time life-changing events, the one that is the most lasting and has the least amount of relapse are programs that are Biblically based.

There are prison programs that are Biblically based that are making lasting changes in the prison population. In Texas, there is a program that has been in prisons for more than ten years and has changed one of the most dangerous prisons in the country into one of the safest. It has been successful in more than one prison and Texas is expanding the program.

Only the Bible can be the basis for permanent change in the lives of folks. In fact, that is one of the goals of this book; to get folks to begin a serious study of the Bible on their own. I challenge any one reading this book - go and begin studying God's word for yourself. Take your problems to Him. Read His word. You will find the answers you seek.

How can I say this with such certainty? The skeptics are already howling. Have you noticed that those who don't believe the Bible is God's word have never actually read God's word, the Bible? They are in that position because deep down they doubt the truth of their conviction and they don't have the courage to test their convictions against God's Word.

Christians on the other hand are encouraged to test their beliefs against God's word. We accept God's word as the final and absolute truth. Skeptics cringe at the thought of an absolute truth.

Life will be miserable for those who have no ultimate truth. They may find companions who share their misguided beliefs (or lack thereof) but that agreement cannot offer the security that is found in real truth. The skeptic will say: 'if you can PROVE the Bible is true then I might believe.'

Let me list the 'proofs' I feel support the truth of the Bible. 1) Changed lives of believers, we have discussed that already. 2) Archaeological evidence/ Historical record. 3) The Bible's continued existence in unaltered form. 4) Fulfilled prophecy.

Chapter Twelve

The archaeological/Historical Record

Throughout history men have wanted to travel to the Holy Land. They wanted to visit the places that are mentioned in the Bible. They want to see them, walk in the dirt of those places, and imagine themselves in the stories they have read about for so many years. People from all walks of life share this desire. Kings and Noblemen have mounted expeditions, governments have paid for archaeologists to research these areas. Treasure have been recovered, early copies of scripture have been found and stories that have been passed down for generations to be shared.

To the skeptic, any city mentioned in the Bible that has an unknown location today is seen as 'proof that that city never existed and the Bible is in error. What the skeptic conveniently overlooks is that each time one of these cities is discovered it ALWAYS confirms the Bible. There is not one instance where the archaeological evidence once found disproves the Bible.

The city of Jericho and its massive walls, discovered and confirming the Bible. The wealth of Solomon. His stables in just ONE location have been discovered, they are massive and there are signs of great wealth. Some say David was really a fictional character. Writings discovered from his era have mentioned not only his name, but him as King.

The skeptic ignores all of these, and there are so many of them. They point to cities, areas, etc. that have not yet been found and say; 'ah-ha, the Bible is wrong '. There is only one explanation for people who think/feel like this.

The Bible says that those who do not believe the truth will at some point be sent a 'strong delusion' to believe the lie. There is a point in each life when God knows beyond that point this person will never believe. This is the point where God will quit sending his people, and his message to you. He knows you are headed for eternal damnation because of the choices you have made. Choices you have willingly made. This would be a terrible position for anyone. It is also a position that is needlessly arrived at. Begin studying the word of God, the Bible. Begin applying the principles in your life. Give your life to him and do it NOW. The historical record supports the truth of the Bible. You have nothing to fear and so much to gain if you will simply humble yourself and come to God. Tell him; 'Lord I don't know if you exist, but if you do I want to know you. Please reveal yourself to me as I begin studying your word. Thank you. '

That is a prayer God will ALWAYS answer. He wants us to know him and he will reveal him- self to those who honestly seek him. The Bible says that 'God is a rewarder of them that diligently seek him'.

We can't leave the discussion on archaeology without having a discussion of the flood and the implications it had on the whole world. One of the arguments against a world-wide flood is Egypt. According to accepted histories their nation began before the flood and continued after the flood with seemingly no disruptions.

This section borrows from and I would like to thank Dr. Elizabeth Mitchell and her work 'Answers 2'. She states that the popular Egyptian chronology that has been historically followed comes from the work of Menetho's history and Sothic history.

In the 3rd Century Menetho compiled a list of Pharos and the length of their reigns. Menetho never intended his work to be a chronological histoly of Egypt and there are even discrepancies that prove this. The Traditional

Dating Method Follows:

Old Kingdom   Dynasties 1-6   2770 B.C.

Great Pyramids   4th Dynasty   2600-2500 B.C.

1st Intermediate Period   Dynasties 7-11 2150-1986 B.C.

Middle Kingdom   Dynasties 12-13   1986-1759 B.C.

2nd Intermediate Period Dynasties 14-17 1759-1525 BC

New Kingdom Dynasties 18-20   1525-1069 BC

3rd Intermediate Period Dynasties 21-25 1069-664 BC

Late Period (Persian) Dynasties 26-31   664-332 BC

Alexander the Great   332-323 BC

Ptolemaic Period   323-30 BC

Roman Period Began 30 BC

**NOTICE THERE ARE TWO SEPARATE BREAKS IN THE 'OFFICIAL' TIME LINE ABOVE THAT TOTALS 520 YEARS!!

People who took the chronology of Menetho assumed all were consecutive and in so doing show the Egyptian empire to be much older than Down says it to be.

Down says that many of the kingdoms mentioned in fact ruled concurrently not consecutively. This was primarily because of the upper and lower kingdoms. When following his guide, the Egyptian kingdoms began around 2150 B.C. which puts it not only after the flood but after the tower of Babel as well!

Mizrail, Noah's grandson is said to have established Egypt around 2188 B.C. This is where his people settled after the population was scattered after the tower of Babel.

The archeological record also supports technology arising with population centers, not ages afterwards as many think. The people scattered from Babel carried their education with them. In fact, it is said in Josephus' writings that Abraham was the one who brought advanced mathematics, knowledge of astronomy, etc. Into Egypt. "For before Abraham came these people were unfamiliar with these palts of learning". Science came from the Chaldeans into Egypt and was probably brought by Abraham in the 4th Dynasty.

The Exodus

Using Down's chronology you can see that Neferhotep was probably the Pharaoh of the Exodus. Neferhotep's mummy was never found (because he died in the Red Sea with his

Army). His son did not succeed him (because he died in the plague of Egypt's first born). He was succeeded by his brother Sobkhotpe IV. This just didn't happen, the parental lineage continued unless there was a tragedy of some sort or no heirs at all.

They have also found mass graves during this period with no tools or utensils as you would normally see - indicating these mass burials were hurriedly done. The whole of Egypt burying their first born at the same time would account for this.

When you use a more accurate time line you can see that there is no conflict with the Bible chronology. In fact, it supports the Bible timeline over and over.

Chapter Thirteen

The Bible's Continued Existence

For thousands of years the Bible was copied by hand. It was a laborious s task. Scribes in Israel took the work so seriously that any mistake made in transcribing the word was not just crossed out or erased. It was removed.

In those days the word was written on scrolls that were rolled up until they were unrolled to be read. They were usually made from some sort of animal skin. If a mistake was made, even if it was the last word or letter on a page - that entire page was cut out and burned. Clean skin sewed in that place and it was re-transcribed. Hand written copies from those days were not allowed to have any errors. That was the only way to protect the integrity of the language as it was copied and handed down from generation to generation.

Since this process took so long for each single copy to be made, and since this was done until the advent of the printing press-you would think that there couldn't be that many copies that existed. You would think that would make it easier for anyone wishing to destroy God's Word.

Efforts to destroy God's word have been made through the centuries and in each case those efforts failed. People were willing to die in order to protect God's word. Is anyone willing to die to protect - Harry Potter? War & Peace? Any secular book? I think not.

What about other religious texts? Let's look at the Koran. Would Muslims die for their religious text? Maybe. They are certainly willing to kill anyone who is destroying their religious text. Christians on the other hand pray for those trying to destroy the Bible instead of killing them. That supports one of the ultimate truths described in the Bible - there is value in God's eye for eve1y human being, not just believers. Our job is to freely share the gospel with them and pray that they will see the truth in God's word and accept Jesus as Lord and Savior.

Yes, historically Christians did persecute non-believers. Were they told to do so in the Bible? Of course not. They were misguided zealots in some cases and in others they were simply drunk with their own power. In either case they were wrong. But these cases have always been used by those looking for an excuse to not believe. Anyone looking for an excuse to not believe in God and his word can find one.

The Dead Sea scrolls were discovered in 1948. There was a copy of the book of Isaiah from the Old Testament that was about 97% complete. It was estimated to be over 900 years old. It was exactly like the book of Isaiah that we know and have in our Bibles today. The integrity of the scripture from before the age of the printing press until now was confirmed. The Bible that we know is the Bible God wanted us to have.

What about different translations? The King James translation was the first widely accepted English translation. Tyndale may have been first but not used worldwide. The King James translation took around 20 years to complete. It was not slapped together quickly. They had the best scholars who had spirited discussions on the specific meaning of ce1tain passages.

Evidently they got it right. It was and still is the standard among which translations have been compared for over 400 years. There are other scholarly translations available

64

today. I believe that translators seeking God's guidance over their efforts were given it.

I also believe that there have been efforts that were done without seeking God's guidance, theirs were efforts to prove a point or viewpoint. Those efforts have been limited in scope and acceptance. In those cases we should use caution. The Bible frames our viewpoints and beliefs - it is not supposed to be the other way around.

In the Book of Revelation God tells us that anyone who changes one dot or tittle in the word will suffer the punishment described in the Book of Revelation s. God takes his word seriously and we should also.

But always remember, it is the seriousness of the transcription that gives us the confidence that we do in fact have the word of God in our hand. The word of salvation and the word of truth. God has given us everything we need to find our salvation. He has given us his forgiveness, His Son and his word. It is up to us now to follow the steps he has laid before us.

Fulfilled Prophecy

God gave us prophecy so that his people would know in advance what is coming. So when it comes and others are idling around in doubt, confusion and fear we can be calm knowing that God is in charge and bringing his plan to fruition.

Prophecy is particularly problematic for the skeptic because they don't know any way to com- bat it; other than to say it had to be written AFTER the fact! No other book in history has had the amount of prophecy that the Bible has. No other book in history has the amount of fulfilled prophecy that the Bible has. The Bible stands alone.

Prophecy is saying in advance what is going to happen, i.e., telling the future before it happens. There have always been fortune tellers and books that claim to be able to tell the future (go to the financial section in any bookstore and see all of the titles that speak of the 'coming economic collapse', etc.).

The Bible test of a prophet is 100% accuracy. When God says something will happen, it will happen. When people say something will happen, they may get it right some of the time but nowhere close to 100% of the time. Skeptics know that. They know 100% accuracy is ONLY possible if God says so. Since they live to plant doubts about the existence of God, prophecy is a threat to them unlike any other.

One way skeptics try and discredit prophecy is to allegorize them. They say you cannot take prophecy literally. By doing this, they can make prophecy relate to or detract from anything they wish. They can make it relate to one event or many separated by years. It's like a magician having the audience look at his left hand while manipulating reality with his right hand.

But the skeptics forget one very important point. God is the same yesterday, today and forever; he is unchanging. If God has literally fulfilled prophecy in the past isn't it logical to assume he will fulfil prophecy literally in the future? Why would he change and allow prophecy to suddenly become allegorical? What could be gained from doing so? All it would do is to cause confusion. The Bible tells us that God is not the author of confusion and doubt, but of a sound mind. It tries to make God do the opposite and be the opposite of who he is. It tries to make God fit OUR definition of him instead of learning who he really is. It tries to make us God.

Isn't that the real reason behind the secular viewpoint? That WE are gods and don't need a God apart from ourselves? Have you heard that lie before? How about the lie from the serpent in the Garden of Eden? I guess King Solomon was right, there is nothing new under the sun.

The skeptics have said that Jesus knowingly made his life 'fit' prophecies so he could claim that he was the messiah. Would any 'man' do that? Jesus only lived 33 years. His ministry began at about the age of 30. So a man would have to be willing to die on a cross in order to be 'worshipped' for three years? If you remember, Jesus was only accepted as messiah by a few, hated by most and probably misunderstood by nearly evelyone. Would you go through that for three years and then voluntarily offer yourself to be crucified for that privilege?

It amazes me how illogical people can become when they are trying to disprove God and his word. It's like the view that God didn't make humans here on the earth. Aliens from another world came here years ago and planted us on this world! Yeah right, that's far more believable.

How could Jesus control his place of birth? Obviously he could not. That means it would have had to be a conspiracy to make Jesus the messiah! Mary and Joseph would have had to hatch the plan to make their son the messiah. It would mean that they planned to travel to Bethlehem for Jesus to be born - BEFORE the census was issued! That was certainly convenient wasn't it?

They would have to be willing to put their lives in danger

to the point of having to flee to Egypt to escape the wrath of the King. Would you make such a trip under those circumstances to sup- port a lie? The skeptics' arguments just keep getting more and more laughable. Are they incapable of thinking their own theories through? Can't they see how ridiculous their theories are before they offer them? They must think the populace is comprised of complete idiots and morons. Unfortunately, that's exactly what they think.

Finally, they can't argue the crucifixion, there is too much evidence for that from other historical sources. That leaves the resurrection. They believe that Jesus didn't die on the cross but was instead drugged to simulate death. The cool of the tomb or an antidote brought by the apostles revived him. If this was the case, where did Jesus go then? What did he do the rest of his life? He couldn't 'live as messiah and enjoy the fruits of his labors'.

Some say his body was simply stolen and reburied elsewhere. The Roman guards would have prevented that unless they were bribed. But they faced death themselves if someone in their charge escaped. How much money would you take to face death?

When you accept or promote a position that is completely illogical and possibly life threatening in order to discredit a position that is logical (even though miraculous), it says that you are probably unstable. Yet, we see them do this time and time again.

Let's look at the Apostle Paul. If Jesus did not rise from the grave he could not have appeared to Paul on the road to Damascus, unless he came as a man and said 'here's the plan'...

Paul endured being shipwrecked and nearly drown; being jai led more than once, being stoned, being beaten, being flogged, etc. Paul was an exceptional man. A Jew, a Roman citizen, schooled by Gamaliel (the Harvard of his day). If a man came to him with a 'plan' what was it that would cause an educated man like Paul to not only endure those trials but to keep the conspiracy quiet? What could the 'plan' offer Paul that would induce him to play a palt? Can you make sense of that? I can assure you Paul would not have made sense of that either.

If on the other hand, Jesus appeared to Paul as is described in the Bible - in a miraculous way. With Jesus telling Paul who he was and that Paul was in fact persecuting Jesus through his persecution of the disciples that Paul was seeking out to punish. Paul became temporarily blinded by this appearance and Jesus told him where to go to get his sight restored. THAT kind of experience would have a lasting impact and Paul's conviction would be seen as a completely normal response to this miraculous intervention in his life by Jesus himself.

We can have similar change in our lives when we accept Jesus as our Lord and Savior. Do it today, please don't wait. None of us knows what tomorrow may bring.

Prophecy is the true north of the Bible. All else can be questioned if you don't have any faith. However, when you see prophecies that have been literally fulfilled time after time over thou- sands of years how can you continue to doubt? Can't you see that such a position can have no basis in a healthy mental state? In light of convincing proof like fulfilled prophecy if you are going to question anything you must question the basis of your own convictions. What is supporting your convictions? If you are honest you will concede that your convictions are based in faulty logic and assumptions. It is time to reassess those convictions and approach the Bible from an unbiased position. Don't be afraid to question yourself, God will give you the answers you need if you approach him sincerely. Start reading your Bible today.

Chapter Fourteen

Why Would a Loving God...? To Make an End of Sin

The answer to the questions we have raised is simply 'to make an end of sin'. A Loving God did everything He has done in the way He did it to make an end of sin. Nothing ever caught God by surprise. He saw the ultimate finish and how good it could be and He knew the path He chose for creation was one that would be appreciated by all as it unfolded and accomplished His will.

The path He chose is one that would not have to be repeated-ever. The lynchpin of His plan was Jesus who died 'once for all' for all of mankind. I do not know why God has chosen to not have a savior for the Angels who sinned. I trust that will become apparent to us in eternity future as we continue our efforts to 'know God '.

God wanted a creation that would voluntarily and freely worship Him as Lord of all, the God of the universe. The Bible tells us that the Angels at present are created on a higher level than man. We are also told that in the future in our glorified form that we will be above the Angels. Man also was given free will - to voluntarily worship God. We can choose to accept Him or not, it is up to us. The Angels had the same choice to make and one third of them chose to rebel with Satan. Sin was originally brought into God's universe - by Satan and the Angels who followed him.

God knew this would happen. Then Satan brought the opportunity of sin to man and Adam did in fact sin. Now sin became a part of mankind. God knew this would happen also. Jesus volunteered to be the savior of mankind from 'before the foundation of the world'.

Once Jesus completed His task sacrificing Himself for mankind, He left the Holy Spirit with us to help us accomplish the most important task of all; sharing the gospel with the whole world. The salvation of mankind rests with us. It is an awe-inspiring responsibility, and a fitting one. Man caused our own downfall and through man God will share the plan of salvation with all men. Isn't it amazing? God will use a puny ant like me to be a part of providing the directions that others need as they seek salvation. He is using you and me to spread the plan!

The skeptics say; 'well we're just pawns being used by God '. If you don't believe in God you don't have a vely high opinion of humans themselves or their worth. I can see how they say we are just pawns - according to them, what else could we be? According to God we are beings of infinite worth, instead of pawns we are in fact the leading characters.

We have been entrusted by the Lord of the Universe with carrying out His will on the earth. As creation moves into the next phase, all creation will have had a chance to see the mercy, forgiveness, sacrifice, gifting, encouragement and freedom that God gave to us. We have had a chance to get a preview of the goodness that is God.

The Angels who remained faithful to God (by choice) saw the dreadful effects of sin. They saw Jesus (their Lord) die an awful death on the cross; they saw God the Father's sorrow as his only Son suffered an extreme death. They experienced the total joy in heaven as Jesus was resurrected and came to heaven having accomplished his mission on earth. Their faith always has been and always will be secure. They know that there is still more to be done to complete the plan. Even so, they long to be able to dine at the marriage supper of the lamb where all believers will celebrate their salvation with a banquet in heaven, hosted by Jesus himself.

The Tribulation period is a period of seven years where man is persecuted by man and where man begins receiving the judgment of God. After this period there is a 1,000 year period where Jesus himself will rule and reign on earth. Men will live longer and sin will be ve1y rare and swiftly dealt with.

At the end of this 1,000 year period Satan will be allowed to tempt humans one last time and believe it or not a portion of those alive at this time will follow him once again. They will be quickly judged as will Satan and his Angels. After this, eternity will begin.

God says in the Bible that he will not 'let insurrection rise a second time'. I read of a gentleman who was transported to heaven for a brief few seconds. As he was taking in the sights and sounds of heaven he realized in his spirit that the sin nature was gone. It was something he just intuitively knew. I agree with that. Our spiritual bodies will have no sin nature.

So the remaining Angels in Heaven will all be sinless. Glorified mankind will all be sinless and sin will be effectively banned for all eternity as there is no sin nature to create a desire to sin in any creature within all of the creation of God's universe. There is no way for sin to rise again. This is all done with creatures that have free will and offer their worship to God voluntarily. No one is forced to worship. God is with us and we are all with him - forever.

This has been the goal of the Lord since creation; to be with man, to have man with him in a sinless, eternal state. None of this took the Lord by surprise. He knew before he created the universe that sin would enter and a savior would be needed. There would be periods of pain and suffering for all involved. But he also knew that those periods of pain and suffering were temporaly. The eternal bliss of a sin free condition far outweighed any temporary suffering and that ALL of our history was necessaly to get us to the sinless state that he sought for the whole of creation.

When you see and understand the big picture it is easy to agree. Lord forgive us of our sins and let you see us as the sinless creatures you initially desired. Sinless only because of the sacrifice of your son Jesus. We accept his sacrifice and hope that we will forever please you.

I hope you prayed that quick prayer. Put your trust in Jesus. Begin reading your Bible. Ask the Lord to open your eyes as you study his word so that you can be equipped by his Holy Spirit to accomplish his will for your life.

Chapter Fifteen

The Appointed Time, Knowing the 'Season'

Jesus was critical of the religious leaders of his day for not knowing the 'spiritual season' and expecting his coming. Prophecy should have led them to see where they were in God's time line.

We too are supposed to be looking for His coming, His second coming. In fact, there is a special crown for believers who are looking for the Return of Jesus! Since we know it is imp01tant for Him that we are looking for Him; let's make it important for us also. There are signs that show us - at least to a generation, where we are on God' timeline.

The Bible says that those who are alive when Jerusalem is restored will be alive to see 'all these accomplished, all prophecy fulfilled'. Jerusalem is sometimes used interchangeably with Israel. In prophecy it says; 'can a nation be born in a day?' Yes, Israel was born in May of 1948 by United Nation Resolution. A nation was literally 'born in a day'.

So, do we begin counting for the last 'generation' at that point? Since Jerusalem is God's city, we should look there. Israel recaptured all of Jerusalem that was not under their control during the 1967 war. It makes more sense to begin the count of our 'generation ' at that point.

There are a number of different lengths of a generation spoken of in the Bible. The most famous that we remember is where the Bible says God has put man's days at 'three score and ten ', 70 years. A generation under judgment is only 40 years. Other generations have been 110 years, 120 years, etc. In the very Old Testament era men lived hundreds and hundreds of years. However, after the flood it has been 'three score and ten ' and has remained remarkably consistent to this day.

The Bible is clear that we should not try and set dates. God will allow us to know the 'season' but not the specific day. In fact, it says that Jesus does not know the specific date, only God the Father. (That's one of my 'heaven questions ' I'd like to ask one day!)

So, if we can know the season or generation, and we think we should start around 1967, then we can logically pose that the second coming of Jesus will be on or before 2037. If we subtract the seven years for the tribulation (which occurs before the second coming) then the rapture can be at any time between now and 2030. That's not ve1y long is it?

Since there are some questions about which time period God will use for a generation are there other clues we can look at to give us more detail? Yes.

The Bible says that on Jesus ' return during the Battle of Armageddon that if he had not come at that time that no flesh would be saved. All of humanity would be killed. Warfare that lethal did not exist until the invention of nuclear weapons. The generation alive in 1967 is the first generation that was born into a world of nuclear weapons.

Our generation is the first generation born into a world with the Nation of Israel in almost 2,000 years! That also fits.

There is an a1my so large that John describes it in the Book of Revelation as being 200 thou- sand, thousand; that's 200 million. In 1969, Mao Se Tong said that China could mount an army of 200 million soldiers. The exact number mentioned in Revelation. I'm sure he didn't check the Bible before making his boast!

A restoration of the Roman Empire. Folks don't like to talk about Europe in this manner, but it too fits. They have a monetaly union now and with the weaker countries causing problems for the more stable countries it is easy to imagine a fiscal crisis demanding a full union. I read recently that Europe is already staffing a standing almy. So far it is small but it is growing.

The European Union was codified by the 'Treaty of Rome '. It started by the same small countries that started the original Roman Empire and has been growing to fill the continent. There was a prophetic list of all Popes written down hundreds of years ago that listed each Pope and some characteristic that was specific to each for identification purposes. It has been exact until this last Pope, (who was the last Pope on the List and supposed to be known as 'Peter the Roman'). This last Pope chose Francis as his papal name, after Francis of Assisi whose real name was ironically, Peter the Roman! While he comes from South America, his parents are both Italian. All we can do is watch. On the list, this last Pope is the one who will reign during the tribulation period.

The rise of militant Islam. There were a few people that saw this coming as early as the 1960's. Most did not give this any serious consideration. The Bible speaks of martyrs who will be beheaded during the tribulation. This was always hard for me to believe as I thought in our 'modem ' world we were beyond such atrocities. But we have all seen the news reports where Muslims have in fact beheaded people as their religion tells them to do.

The three main religions of the world; Christians, Jews and

Muslims are all expecting the arrival of their messiah. Christians expect the return of Christ, the Jews expect their Messiah, and the Muslims expect the 12th Maddi. In fact, it seems the whole world whether folks are religious or not have a sense that some sort of end is near and some sort of change is coming.

Jesus said that believers would be 'hated for my name's sake'. He told us not to worry because the world 'hated him first'. I didn't think I would see an America where Jesus was hated in my lifetime. I thought that would happen when all believer s are taken out of this world through the rapture. It seems I was wrong.

'Separation of church and state' has been purposely misused to do just that. The phrase 'separation of church and state' does not appear in our founding documents. It was a phrase used by Thomas Jefferson in a personal letter. You can see in the first Amendment to our Constitution it says: 'Congress shall make no law regarding the establishment of any religion or prohibiting the free exercise thereof' those who oppose the Lord always point to the 'establishment ' clause and conveniently forget the second part free exercise of religion.

We accept the Bible as the inspired word of God. We have an example of his Holy Spirit guiding the process to give us his word in the way he wanted us to have it.

I believe there have been other instances of divine intervention throughout history - this is just MY OPINION. The Magna Carta. Our Constitution and founding documents. 200 years has been the historical limit for democratic forms of government. We have passed that and are still counting. Our Constitution has taken some hits and is bruised, but it is still the over-riding law of the land.

Handel's Messiah is one of the few songs that man has written that we may actually hear someday in Heaven. God does show himself to us in many ways.

I mention all of this because another characteristic of those alive at the time of Christ's return is men 'calling evil good and good evil'. A point in time where things are literally turned upside down. References to God and Jesus are being opposed in places we never thought would happen; in our military and the air force. We see Christmas called Winter Break in our schools and during Christmas, stores who try and ignore 'the reason for the season'.

Having our government and prominent leaders say we can have 'freedom of worship ' instead of 'freedom of religion ' as described in our constitution. It may seem a small difference to most but it is not. Freedom to worship means just inside our homes and churches-but not in the public square. A major political party in a recent national election actually voted to remove any reference to God in their political platform!

It seems there are new news reports every week of another case where someone complained and found a sympathetic judge to agree with their viewpoint to try and eliminate God in another arena. This would all be stunning on its own. If you view it as a reference on God's timeline you can see that time is short. People are calling good evil and evil good, nearly every day somewhere in our country.

The Bible also says that the last generation before the Return of Christ would be one where drug use was rampant. I used to think that reference was only to illegal drugs (and yes, the use of illegal drugs is rampant). But it refers to legal drugs. The Greek word Pharmacia is where we get our word 'pharmacy'. We have to be the most drugged generation that has ever lived. Doctors prescribe drugs for our children who are mostly just doing things that children do. When you watch TV at night the companies that seem to spend the most on television ads are the drug companies. Every condition is abbreviated and they have just the drug to help the condition. We even have drugs for our pets!

Sexual immorality and impurity is rampant. The internet for all the good it can provide has opened a Pandora's Box where our kids on average by age eleven have been exposed to inappropriate things on line. Sexual immorality is another sign of the last generation.

The Bible says that men will 'worship the creation rather than the creator '. Yes, we are told to be stewards of the earth. But never to 'worship' the earth as many in the environmental movement do. This is another sign of the last generation.

Wars and Rumors of wars. I don't think there was a time during the 20th Century when there was NOT a war somewhere in the world; including two World Wars, Korea, Vietnam, Ethnic Rivalries in Eastern Europe, the Middle East and Africa, the list just goes on and on. But with all of this Jesus said; 'the end is not yet '. But it is a sign.

Natural disasters! Primarily earthquakes which have increased exponentially in frequency and severity-just like Jesus said they would. The environmentalists try and tie all of it back to 'climate change ' (they don't say global warming anymore because-it is not warming!). If they knew their Bible they would know it is not 'climate change ' but 'prophecy change'!

I am not a mathematician. I do know that the odds increase geometrically when you add item after item all happening at the same time. Look at all the signs around us: The establishment of the Nation of Israel.

The Revived Roman Empire via the European Union. The global rise of militant Islam. Upside down values, i.e., calling good evil and calling evil good. Sexual Immorality. Increase in knowledge and speed of communication, speed of travel. Nuclear Weapons. The Weakening of America. Global Financial Problems. Computers, the internet. (knowledge increasing). Natural Disasters. Space Exploration, satellites, star wars, (signs in the sun, moon and stars). The rise of countries in Asia as world powers, (Kings of the East). The 'falling away' of some in the Christian faith. The Jewish intent to rebuild the Temple by 2025. Scoffers and Bible skeptics.

The odds of any two or three of these happening in a single generation would be high. The odds of all of these happening in our generation are beyond calculation. Yet, this is what is happening.   It can't be by coincidence.

Americans have been insulated from the world for the most part. We are woefully unaware of what is happening in other countries around the world. I think we are at that point because we don't feel that what happens in other countries really affects us.

I hope you will realize that what is happening around the world is happening to fulfil prophecy as it unfolds. If this is true then we need to be aware of what is happening in order to be watchful for the return of Jesus. We need to be aware so we won't be caught off-guard like those who were unaware at his first coming.

Chapter Sixteen

A Strong Delusion

The Bible says that unbelievers will be sent a strong delusion in order to believe 'the lie'. It will be so strong that only the 'vely elect' will not be fooled. The rest of the world will be fooled.

I realize this chapter may be controversial and that I may lose some readers here. I ask you to read this with an open mind. As our future unfolds remember this discussion. If I am right then these words could help you keep your salvation.

There is a coming event that will be so spectacular, so 'miraculous ' on its surface that most all of the whole world will believe it. I ask you to think for a moment. With all the different religions on earth, the different ethnic peoples on earth, different education levels, different economic levels, different ages, different experiences and maturity levels; what sort of event could command the attention of everyone and the absolute belief of almost everyone?

It would have to be the appearance of the Lord. But who's Lord? The Jewish Messiah? The return of Christ? The 12th Maddi? Alien ancestors? We are being 'prepped ' for the lie now. This preparation has been going on for decades. In fact, there is even a television show 'promoting' it - albeit unknowingly I think. That show is 'Ancient Aliens '. It amazes me how unbelievers in the Lord can be believers in a story that aliens came here eons ago and 'planted ' humans on earth!

Look at the world media. They hate Jesus. The Jewish Messiah is spoken of in ethereal terms like it is a fable. The

12th Maddi is rarely even spoken of outside the Muslim world. But the story they promote is the story of and a belief in 'intelligent life in the universe outside of earth'; aliens.

NASA, SETI and other agencies and governments are actively seeking signs of other life in the universe. Theories abound and while none have been proved they continue to demand academic respect. That respect if not given can ruin careers.

There are celtain 'agendas' that are pushed. Aliens are close to the top of the list. There has not been any discovery outside the earth that supports this in any way. However, there is a phenomena within the bounds of earth that does support that view, UFO's.

President Reagan said in a speech to the United Nations that a UFO landing would unite the world like no other event in history. It would put an end to our petty squabbling and make us realize all that humans have in common. Does anyone believe the world has changed to the point where Reagan's statement would be untrue today?

So, are UFO's real? Yes, but not as you think them to be. I enjoy watching Star Wars and Star Trek as much as anyone. But the reality is our universe is just too big to be explored in such a manner as depicted on these shows.

These shows use different terms to describe travel beyond the speed of light because they know travel at faster than light speed is the only way to have the ability to explore the universe. Whether it is warp factor or 'jumping to light speed ' we as an audience being entertained accept it.

Reality is quite different. Do you know that electricity and light both travel at the same speed? 186,000 miles per second! Does anyone think that is a coincidence? There are limits and boundaries that God established when he made the universe. These were established to create order in the universe. Order that was structured in such a way that when God looked at the universe he made he could say it is good.

If light speed is in fact a barrier and space ship exploration is limited because of the size of the universe, then the possibility of aliens visiting us in 'space ships' is out of the equation. So how do we explain UFO's? What are they?

UFO's are inter dimensional. That is the only explanation. A number of researchers have already reached this opinion. However, they don't know where to go from this point.

The Bible speaks of inter dimensional beings, they are called Angels. We know the angels who remained loyal to the Lord still serve him and do his bidding. The Bible calls them 'ministering spirits sent to serve'. They serve the Lord by helping us. They may bring a message or protection. They are ready to be used by the Lord at any time. There is no need for them to create a 'delusion ' so that we would believe a 'lie'. The Bible says God cannot lie and he would never send servants to us to offer a lie. So UFO's cannot be loyal angels of the Lord.

That leaves fallen angels as the only explanation. Fallen angels are enemies of the Lord and loyal to Satan. They will do all in their power to try and ruin God's plan of salvation for mankind and to raise Satan up as the savior and lord of mankind.

How are UFO's promoting this vision? They are conditioning mankind to accept 'aliens'. I believe that at some point in the near future that these fallen angels will make a 'landing' and have formal contact with humans.

They will spread the lie that they came ages ago and populated the earth with humanity. They will promote Satan as the real creator of mankind. This will be 'the lie' that Jesus warned us about in the Bible.

You don't think it could happen? Look at the movie 'Independence Day'. In that movie the aliens were evil and immediately began destroying our world. Imagine a similar scenario where the aliens behaved in a benevolent manner. They brought new technologies and medicines, solved our economic problems on a world-wide basis, cured cancer, etc. How would they be received? How would the media report the alien story and their agenda? Yep, they would buy it hook, line and sinker.

Let's look at all of this spiritually now. The Bible tells us that anyone who receives the 'mark' of the beast in their hand or forehead will immediately lose their hope of salvation and will be damned to hell. Harsh isn't it? So harsh that we need to be fully informed about the mark so we won't lose our salvation.

Many have wondered over the years if people could be 'forced' to take the mark and lose their salvation. I don't think so. People have lost their physical lives in the past for the testimony of Jesus and there will be many who will lose their physical lives in the coming tribulation period for their testimony of Christ. But ALL of those win a special place in heaven because of that sacrifice and their salvation is secure.

People who take the mark in the future will do so voluntarily because they perceive it to be a benefit to themselves. Most folks are not believer s and they have no idea what they are dealing with. They have no idea that receiving the mark will damn them to hell.

So what could the benefits be? 1) The ability to buy and sell goods, services and food. We are soft. We have had things so good economically in our country I wonder how long we could hold out having to rely solely on the Lord for our food. The Bible tells us that no believer will go hungry. Do we believe him or not?

The Bible says that in this period it will be like in the days of Noah. The characteristics of that time include: sin and violence (terrorism), the Nephalim, and extended life spans.

Now suppose these 'aliens' offered not just the ability to buy and sell if you take their mark but also an extended life span (maybe hundreds of years) without sickness. Do you think that would tempt many to receive the mark?

Receiving the mark will be voluntary not forced. People will be happy to do so. They will think they are entering a new golden age of humanity. Accepting the mark will show allegiance to the alien leader, i.e., Satan, who will after a time reveal himself as the beast he is. But by this time it will be too late to reverse your decision and remove the mark and your public statement of allegiance.

The 'mark' may well be some sort of implant in the hand or fore head. Why is damnation the only option God gives to those who have received the mark? I think because the mark may in fact change human DNA into demonic DNA. With human DNA we have a sin nature. With demonic DNA we become sin and that's why the door of heaven is closed to those with the mark.

Christian researcher and author L.A. Marzulli has studied the Nephalim and the coming deception for years. (I urge all readers to look him up on line and listen to his teaching. You can find some teaching videos and interviews on You

Tube.) They have actually helped people who have been abducted by aliens (demons) to have their implants surgically removed. These implants were in essence microcomputers that are about 100 times more powerful than our fastest computers. One of the doctors was asked what these implants could potentially be doing once they are inside a human. His response was 'changing their DNA '.

The Nephalim were the offspring of the fallen angels and human women from the time before the flood of Noah. If allowed to continue, their lineage of demonic DNA would have infected all of humanity and prevented a pure line for the savior, Jesus, to be born. The flood was the death sentence for them and their offspring. Noah's line was still pure so the human race was once again untainted after the flood.

God made man in his own image. Satan tries to counterfeit all of God's creation. In this case, Satan wants to have man in HIS image, not God's image. This is the purpose behind the attempt to change man's DNA into some sort of demonic DNA.

This is also the reason that anyone who accepts the mark will automatically lose any hope of salvation just like the Nephalim from the days of Noah). If they accept the mark voluntarily and it changes their pure human DNA into some sort of demonic DNA, then God cannot allow them into heaven. Their demonic DNA is sin. God cannot co-exist with sin in any manner. Sin in any form cannot be allowed to enter heaven.

The lie is: 'you can be as gods '. The aliens were once like us and evolved into their 'God status'. By accepting the mark and starting on that journey, we too can become gods.

The same lie that Satan told Eve in the Garden of Eden. New Agers are you listening?

I believe that if you are middle age or younger and in good health, that you may vely well see this or some other similar scene play out in our lifetime. You need to know what could be coming and be prepared. You need to remember this and not be fooled by the events that are com- mg.

Remember, the reason God gave us prophecy is so that his people will know in advance the things that are coming. So we can be prepared for the things that are coming. So we will not be caught by surprise.

Our churches should be teaching this to their congregations. Many faithful followers have read and understood their Bibles and may be ready to face the upcoming event, the lie. Many others may not be ready.

I once again ask all readers to begin studying their Bible and ask God for wisdom as you read and study. Ask him to show you the knowledge you will need to not be deceived, to keep your salvation secure, and to be able to lead others into the knowledge they will need to not be deceived in the coming events.

Some years ago Jerry Fallwell was asked in an interview if he thought the antichrist was alive somewhere on the ealth. If you believe that time is short, the obvious answer is yes. There was a firestorm in the media! Why? Because if the antichrist is real then the Bible is true. If the Bible is true then there is a creator God above and apalt from creation. This means their world- view, i.e., evolution is false and they know they will in fact have to one day be judged by the Lord of all creation. That thought scares them to death.

(As it would anyone who is not saved by the blood of Jesus).

The Bible does not tell us how the antichrist enters our world. Copying Christ and being born of a virgin? Possibly. Opening the hatch of a spacecraft and saying 'here I am' - possibly. Jesus told us to be on guard for the coming deception. Believers will recognize it when they see it. The alien angle is simple another possibility that may require us to be prepared.

Chapter Seventeen

Why Would a Loving God...?

Because He Loves You.

We have covered a lot of ground even though this is a short book. We have talked of the pre-universe creation, sin beginning ages ago in Heaven; the creation of the universe, the fall of man, history of mankind and the efforts of Satan to thwart God's plan of redemption for man. We finally looked at the potential coming events which are the culmination of Satan's plan, his last hurrah to try and deceive mankind into losing their salvation.

The good news is, Satan loses! He cannot win. He knows it but he thinks his reward is taking as many humans with him as he can.

This path is a long one for humans. It is only a short path for the Lord, but a costly one. The path required Him to allow his Son Jesus, to become sin and to be crucified to reconcile man to God. God did this because He loves us. Each and every one of us is a beautiful creation. He wants us to be with him forever and was willing to offer Jesus in our stead to make that possible.

Could you love like that? Can you even understand a love like that? I can't. But I can offer my most sincere Thank You to the Lord. I can ask him to help make me the man he wants me to be and to do the task he wants me to do.

To be courageous in sharing the good news with others; friends, family and strangers alike when the opportunity arises. To live a life he will one day say; 'well done thou good and faithful servant'.

Remember the Apostle Paul who said: "Eye has not seen and ear has not heard the glories that await us in Heaven".

May we all see and hear the glories of heaven someday! See you on the other side!!

Printed in Great Britain
by Amazon.co.uk, Ltd.,
Marston Gate.